GOD IS INTERESTED
IN YOUR MARRIAGE

Path to a Successful, Happy Christian Marriage

Daniel Ukadike Nwaelene, ThD.

GOD IS INTERESTED IN YOUR MARRIAGE

Path to a Successful, Happy Christian Marriage

Daniel Nwaelene Books, LLC
190 Palisade Ave #4D
Yonkers, NY 10703, USA
www.danielnwaelenebooksllc.com
914 282-0120

Because of the dynamic nature of the Internet, any web addresses or links contained in this book may have changed since publication and may no longer be valid. The views expressed in this work are solely those of the author and do not necessarily reflect the views of the publisher, and the publisher hereby disclaims any responsibility for them.

ISBN (eBook): 979-8-9939253-0-1
ISBN (Paperback): 979-8-9922386-8-6
ISBN (Hardback): 979-8-9922386-9-3

DEDICATION:

To all married couples who are still living,

or lived together

longer than forty years.

Abbreviations of Bible Versions Quoted in This Book:

Amplified Bible	- AMP
Authorized (King James) Version	- AKJV
King James Version	- KJV
English Standard Version	- ESV
New American Standard Bible	- NASB
New English Translation	- NET
New International Version	- NIV
New King James Version	- NKJV
New Living Translation	- NLT
Revised Standard Version	- RSV

PREFACE

Are you enjoying or enduring your marriage?

Someone has said that a healthy, prosperous, and happy marriage gives a taste on earth of heaven, while on the contrary, a failing, unhappy marriage gives a taste of hell on earth (though in the real sense of it, no matter how terrible life may be on earth, no situation can be compared to 'life' in unquenchable hell fire). Much as it is true that any person outside a marriage is not party to it, the only One that is not an intruder is the One Whose idea marriage was – GOD.

He watches every step taken in the marriage; He dictates the tune and expects the couple, without coercion, to dance to it. It is, therefore, great counsel to "Trust in the Lord with all your heart, And lean not on your own understanding; 6 In all your ways acknowledge Him, And He shall direct your paths." (Proverbs 3:5-6 NKJV).

Until, and unless you are married, you have no marriage experience. Marriage experience does not come by reading books or hearing stories; and Godly wisdom comes from GOD and His Word.

It is God that gives you power to make wealth (Deuteronomy 8:18)[1], and according to Psalm 75:5-7 AKJV, "Lift not up your

---

[1] Deuteronomy 8:18 NKJV "And you shall remember the Lord your God, for *it is* He who gives you power to get wealth, that He may establish His covenant which He swore to your fathers, as *it is* this day.

horn on high: speak *not with* a stiff neck. [6] For promotion *cometh* neither from the east, nor from the west, nor from the south. [7] But God *is* the judge: he putteth down one, and setteth up another." God is the One that gives financial and/or material prosperity."

Two of the Bible passages that tell that it is God that gives children are Psalm 127:3: "children are a gift from God." And Psalm 113:9 – "He grants the barren woman a home, Like a joyful mother of children. Praise the Lord!"

So, you must trust, and depend on, the Lord for all these blessings of marriage.

It is God that also gives long life and good health, both of which are necessary in a successful and happy marriage, and may occasionally be taken for granted. Read these: Deuteronomy 32:39 NKJV "'Now see that I, *even* I, *am* He, And *there is* no God besides Me; I kill and I make alive; I wound and I heal; Nor *is there any* who can deliver from My hand."

Exodus 23:25-26 NKJV "So you shall serve the Lord your God, and He will bless your bread and your water. And I will take sickness away from the midst of you. [26] No one shall suffer miscarriage or be barren in your land; I will fulfill the number of your days."

Psalm 91:16 NKJV "With long life I will satisfy him, And show him My salvation."

Proverbs 10:27 NKJV "The fear of the Lord prolongs days, But the years of the wicked will be shortened."

Bear in mind that God determines what long life is for everyone. But trust Him for long life for you, your spouse and children.

The number, Three is said to be "the magic number." Vine's Dictionary says it "is regarded by many as a number sometimes symbolically indicating fullness of testimony or manifestation, as in the three persons of the Godhead"[2] –

- The Trinity: Father, Son and Holy Spirit.

It can also symbolize the following:

- Time: Past, present and future;

- Natural cycle: birth, life and death; etc.

Your marriage needs to be a triune unit for it to be perfect as follows: husband wife and God, with God at/as the Base of the triangle. If you do, He watches and upholds the marriage. If God is present in your marriage, it behooves you both to live godly, and honor Him in and with your lives and the marriage.

This book, which was initially to be developed for a sermon, therefore assumes that the man and woman in this marriage are

---

[2] W.E. Vine. Vine's Complete Expository Dictionary of Old and New Testament Words. (Nashville, TN: Thomas Nelson Publishers, 1984), 631.

children of God as per John 1:11-13[3], who understand that a believer shouldn't be unequally yoked together with unbelievers as per 2 Corinthians 6:14 AKJV: "Be ye not unequally yoked together with unbelievers: for what fellowship hath righteousness with unrighteousness? and what communion hath light with darkness?"

Someone has inferred from the above Bible verse that when you, a child of God, are married to an unbeliever, the devil – the father of the unbeliever – is your father-in-law. In that case, you and your spouse may not have exactly the same agenda and lifestyle. Light and darkness cannot successfully go or operate together.

---

[3] John 1:11-13 AKJV He came unto his own, and his own received him not. [12] But as many as received him, to them gave he power to become the sons of God, *even* to them that believe on his name: [13] which were born, not of blood, nor of the will of the flesh, nor of the will of man, but of God.

Fig. 1 The Godly Marriage Triangle

This book is purposed to draw your attention to the place of the almighty God in your marriage. God is able and willing to guide you to the right spouse for you (if still single), help you through marriage difficulties – providing solutions for you, save your marriage from breaking up and heal wounds arising from disagreements that could lead to separation or divorce.

Divorce is death of a marriage. The Scriptures says, "Jesus said unto her, I am the resurrection, and the life: he that believeth in me, though he were dead, yet shall he live: 26 and whosoever liveth and believeth in me shall never die." (John 11:25-26). Jesus Christ raised the dead back to life and is able to resurrect a dead marriage and save a dying one if you have faith in Him to do so.

This book is, therefore, targeted at people contemplating marriage, husband and wife considering separation or divorce, divorced husbands and wives, young people (single and married), marriage counselors, parents, and teachers.

God hates divorce. For this reason, it is essential to go into marriage, determined and prepared to avoid any circumstances that could lead to divorce, trusting GOD to give you marital bliss and success.

GOD Is Interested in Your Marriage is meant to help with shaky marriages to understand that their marriages can be saved, assure prospective couples that their marriages could be successful, and hence go ahead boldly into marriage, settle down and enjoy each other. Also, to help couples whose marriages are at the brink of hitting the rocks, and provide some guide for other members of the family.

Some people had wondered why in my earlier books I fully quoted Bible verses and passages, a principle also applied in this one. The reason is to create opportunities for the reader to have access to the *raw* Bible information. I have observed that not many readers of books stop to check references. By fully stating the Bible references in this book, you are provided with the full information about the idea referenced.

I appreciate that you are reading this book and will appreciate you more when you patiently read it to the end with an open mind and tell someone else about the book. Thank you. And may GOD bless you and increase your knowledge of Him, giving you peace in your family. AMEN.

Rev. Daniel U. Nwaelene, ThD.

August 2023.

ACKNOWLEDGMENTS

First and foremost, all thanks and praise to the almighty GOD, for the inspiration and enabling grace to get this work published – giving the ideas, providing the strength and conducive environment. Lord, thank You.

No one person is a repository of all knowledge. That is why, in the process of putting this work together, researches and references were conducted or made to other authors' works. Most or all of these works in the form of books, journals, Bible commentaries, Dictionaries, Internet articles and so on, were duly acknowledged as footnotes in the body of the book, and in the Bibliography. I wish to hereby sincerely appreciate the authors of such materials so cited or quoted from for permitting me to share in their intellectual properties. Thank you all very much.

Thanks also to my wife, Patricia for her assistance and cooperation all through the periods of my work on this book. May the Lord bless you again and again.

Thanks also go to ---- (*the publishing company*) ------- for helping to edit and publish this book.

Finally, many thanks to you for acquiring and reading the book, without which the whole effort to produce the book would have been in futility. God bless you too.

BOOKS BY THE AUTHOR

1. JESUS CHRIST: Savior, Judge and King of the World

Originally published by: WestBow Press Year: 2017.
www.westbowpress.com Tel.: +1 866 928 1240.
Re-published by: Bookside Press www.booksidepress.com –
Year: 2024.
Tel. 1 877 741 8091.

2. ACTING MOVIE SCRIPTS OR FULFILLING
   PROPHECIES?

Originally Published by: Christian Faith Publishing, Inc. – Year:
2018.
www.christianfaithpublishing.com
Re-published by: Daniel Nwaelene Books – Year: 2024
https://danielnwaelenebooksllc.com/ Tel: +1 914 920 9862.

3. FAMILY STRUCTURE BY CHOICE: A Defense of
   Traditional Marriage Structure

Originally published by: iUniverse Publishing - Year: 2020
www.iuniverse.com Tel.: +1 800 288 4677
Re-published by: Gotham Books, Inc
https://gothambooksinc.com Year: 2022 Tel: +1 307 404 7800.

4. GOD IS INTERESTED IN YOUR MARRIAGE: Path to a
   Successful, Happy Christian

Marriage
Originally published by: Gotham Books, Inc. - Year: 2024
https://gothambooksinc.com Tel: +1 307 404 7800.

5. MONEY, POWER AND SEX: The Implication of Money,
Power and Sex In The Downfall of People
Published by Daniel Nwaelene Books, LLC. – Year: 2025
https://danielnwaelenebooksllc.com/ Tel: +1 914 920 9862.

FOREWORD

Dr. Daniel Nwaelene's Book "God is Interested in Your Marriage" is a review of the biblical bases for marriage. In this work Dr. Nwaelene elevates the purpose for marriage above the contemporary societal anthropological, social, ethical or religious argumentations for the union between man and wife. By anchoring his discourse in the biblical supports for marriage he posits that the institution was divinely created and sanctioned by God, therefore God has an eternal interest in "Marriage." Dr. Nwaelene provides practical ways in which marriages can be successful and avoid the pitfalls that lead to many of the failures encountered in marital relationships. The book gives an exhaustive list of biblical text that allows the reader to encounter God's purpose for marriage. I recommend that the book can be used as a guide for couples contemplating marriage, or a source material for marriage counseling by pastors and Christian therapists. This is a satisfying literary work that all readers will find enjoyable, uplifting, and rewarding, as well as, restore our confidence in marriage as the crowning act of God's creative works.

By

Rev. Dr. Nigel O. Cole
Pastor Community Baptist Church.
Yonkers. New York. USA.
(Doctor of Ministry from the New York Theological Seminary).

TABLE OF CONTENT

Chapter 1

INTRODUCTION

There is an opening address that was common at most church weddings until recently. It reads as follows[4]:

Dearly beloved, we are gathered together here in the sight of God to join together this man and woman in holy matrimony. It is an honorable estate, instituted of God, signifying unto us the mystical union that is between Christ and His Church, that holy estate Christ adorned and beautified with His presence and first miracle in Cana of Galilee. It is commended in the Scriptures to be honorable among all, and therefore is not by any to be entered into unadvisedly or lightly, but reverently, discretely, advisedly, soberly and in the fear of God. Into this holy estate these two persons present come now to be joined. If any man can show just cause why they may not be lawfully be joined together, let him now speak or else hereafter forever hold his peace.

Subsequently the minister conducting the wedding leads the couple to make a commitment to each other thus:

(*To the groom*): [*groom's name*], wilt thou take this woman to be your wedded wife, to live together after God's

---

[4] The Pastor's Handbook, Revised KJV Ed. (Chicago, IL: Wing Spread Publishers, 2003), 45

ordinance in the holy estate of matrimony? Wilt thou love her, comfort her, honor and keep her, in sickness and in health, and forsaking all others, keep thee only unto her so long as you both shall live?"[5]

The groom will respond, "I will."

{The same question is posed to the bride regarding the man.}

After the woman has been officially handed over to the man to be married to him, each of the couple respectively makes the other avow as follows:

"I, [groom's name]* take thee, [bride's name]** to be my wedded wife#, to have and to hold from this day forward, for better, for worse, for richer, for poorer, in sickness and in health, to love and to cherish, till death us do part, according to God's holy ordinance; and thereto do I give thee my pledge")[6]

{After the man says his vow to the woman, the woman does hers, changing *groom's name to the bride's; ** bride's to the groom's name, and wife# to husband.}

This gradually culminates in the minister's pronouncement or declaration of the couple as husband and wife as follows: "Those whom God has joined together let no man put asunder.

---

[5] ibid.
[6] ibid, 46.

Forasmuch as [groom's name] and [bride's name] have consented together in holy matrimony and have witnessed the same before God and this company , and thereto have given their pledge, each to the other, and have declared the same in giving and receiving rings, and by joining hands, I pronounce that they are husband and wife, in the name of the Father and of the Son and of the Holy Spirit. Amen."[7]

From this point forward the man and his wife are married before God, witnessed by the people present, and nothing and nobody is allowed or expected to separate them (not even the couple themselves), except inevitable death.

Like many other people, I did not catch the depth and full implications of the marriage vow until about a year later, during another couple's wedding at which I followed as they exchanged their vows. Then when I got home after that wedding I picked and read through my wedding program. It was then that my vow to my wife spoke to me. It is therefore, advisable for married couples to revisit their marriage vows from time to time individually and jointly, to remind themselves of what they said to each other when the love between them was hot, highly potent and "intoxicating." Re-living your wedding has a sobering effect, helping to douse tension and subdue the urge for

---

[7] ibid, 49-50.

divorce or separation - and prevent you from saying "cursed be the day I met you." It should always be "thanks to God for the day I met you."

It is necessary to recount your joy and how many people had joy in their hearts, and how glory was given to God the day of your wedding provided it was God that joined you to gather.[8] The same God is interested in your union, loves to bless, uphold and prosper it if you let him.

Your marriage can be great, if you allow the Author to be present, be in charge and be your Consultant.

---

[8] The Bible says that those whom God has joined together should not be separated. It implies that there may be couples that God has not joined together. The devil is capable of joining people. So also, can money and other authorities not God. For this reason, couples should pray through before getting to the point of "I do."

CHAPTER TWO
WHAT MARRIAGE IS

Until recently, all definitions of marriage principally described it as, the coming together into a union of a man and a woman [9] for the purposes of procreation, companionship, and protection against immorality.

This implies the separation of two adults or young adults - man and woman - from their parents, agreeing to become one, and are joined by an agency of government empowered to do so. Under normal circumstances, the parents of the couple (if living) approve of the marriage before a body goes ahead to formally join the man and woman.

In some communities, approval of a proposed union of a man and woman by their parents is all that is needed for the traditional rulers of the community to formally join them in marriage.

In some other communities joining is performed by a religious body such as Church, mosque or Temple. There are communities where parental consent does not matter to the marriage agency, so long as the man and woman are of

---

[9] In some societies people of the same sex are now allowed to be lawfully married and practice homosexuality, especially in America and Europe.

a certain minimum age - in other words, adults - such as 18 years of age.

When married, the couple become husband and wife and it becomes lawful for them to engage in sexual intercourse and bear children. Generally, before a marriage is consummated there are processes that take place. Otherwise, a man does not just meet a woman and gets married to her. There is a period of dating, then courtship and engagement. These constitute times for learning/studying and knowing each other, notwithstanding that studying to master each other continues even throughout the marriage, which may span many years. A preacher once said, "My wife and I have been married 40 years, and we are still discovering each other."

H. Norman Wright quoted from *The Mystery of Marriage* by Mike Mason as follows: "Marriage partners may be thought of as astronauts of society – the daring explorers who do all the test flying in a sort of on-going experiment in the most radical fringes of human relations. Naturally there are many crashes, many casualties in this stratosphere of intimacy."[10]

It should be noted that cool habitation is not marriage. Cohabitation is the instance of two people living together,

---

[10] H. Norman Wright. The Premarital Counseling Handbook. (Chicago: Moody Press, 1992), 10.

being not married, but in many cases doing what married couples do. The danger in cohabitation before marriage, just like getting married because of a resultant, unplanned-for pregnancy, it usually ends in a divorce full stop nothing new is anticipated to make the wedding exciting. Same as the immediate post wedding days.

CHAPTER THREE
ORIGIN OF MARRIAGE

Marriage was originated and ordained by the almighty God. After God created man and all animals none of the animals was fit for companionship as God felt it was not good for the man to remain alone and lonely. Notwithstanding that some people these days like to keep pets in place of a human partner contrary to God's arrangement, a pet cannot fill a human gap. Genesis 2:20-25 NKJV tells the story:

"So Adam gave names to all cattle, to the birds of the air, and to every beast of the field. But for Adam there was not found a helper comparable to him. [21] And the Lord God caused a deep sleep to fall on Adam, and he slept; and He took one of his ribs, and closed up the flesh in its place. [22] Then the rib which the Lord God had taken from man He made into a woman, and He brought her to the man.

[23] And Adam said:

"This *is* now bone of my bones
And flesh of my flesh;
She shall be called Woman,
Because she was taken out of Man."

[24] Therefore a man shall leave his father and mother and be joined to his wife, and they shall become one flesh. [25] And they were both naked, the man and his wife, and were not ashamed.

Because marriage is God's creation, he supports and sustains it. Of course, there are minimum standards set for every marriage – consisting of the husband, the wife, the children and servant. We shall look into these standards later.

Understanding the origin of marriage should help you to appreciate the sacredness of sanctity of it. Because God is its Author, like He is of life, every marriage is meant to be handled with honor and respect in honor of the Author. In Hebrews 13:4 the word of God says, "Marriage *is* honorable among all, and the bed undefiled; but fornicators and adulterers God will judge." But unfortunately, there are some spouses who treat their marriages with disrespect, dishonor, or some carefree attitude. Such people treat their spouses as if they are just friends, and feel they can relate with other people as they relate with their marriage partners. Respect for your spouse breeds love and brings honor to the Author of marriage - God.

CHAPTER FOUR
IMPORTANCE OF MARRIAGE

Occasionally you find people who do things because they see others do. On the other hand, some people get into some situations or activities accidentally. Marriage is serious business. No wonder it is a major life's event that is seriously celebrated by the couple, having been initiated by them, with them as participants in the ceremonies. Birth and death celebrations are initiated and celebrated on your behalf by others like your parents. Recently I read of a woman who got married at the age of 68, and was quoted as saying that her joy knew no bounds. So, what is so important about marriage? Let us consider nine reasons: -

(1) Perpetuation of Human Race.

   After creating man and making him a help meet fit for him God blessed them and commanded them to be fruitful and multiply, and replenish the earth. God, who also created all other things on in heaven and earth by word of mouth, could have spoken all other human beings into being to populate the world. But rather He chose to let mankind beget more/others. To God, therefore, marriage is the vehicle for achieving this program of procreation and perpetuation of mankind. This is also a proof that marriage other than of a man and a woman is not in consonance with the will of God for mankind. God makes no mistakes. He plans/ planned all things well. He is perfect as Jesus described Him when He said, "Therefore you shall be perfect, just as your Father in heaven is perfect." (Matthew 5:48 NKJV).

(2) Life Partnership.

Marriage provides lifelong partnership for the couple for all life's issues, events and situation. At the end of each day of activities, there is someone there and trusted with whom to share experience and burdens. Joys and pains are shared between the two to lighten the burden. The preacher recorded in Ecclesiastes 4:9- 11 NKJV "Two *are* better than one, Because they have a good reward for their labor. [10] For if they fall, one will lift up his companion.

But woe to him *who is* alone when he falls, For *he has* no one to help him up.

[11] Again, if two lie down together, they will keep warm;

But how can one be warm *alone?*"

(3) Control In Temptation.

Marriage helps couples to control themselves and stand in the face of sexual temptation. Notwithstanding that people cheat and commit adultery, remembering being a married person presents grounds for withdrawal.

(4) Foundation of Family.

Marriage is the beginning of the family and it is important to note that the family is the nucleus of any society - the church, community and nation – being that parents are the primary shapers of their children especially in areas of speaking, morality, behaving in public, how to relate with other people, and so on.

(5) Marriage Unifies.

Marriage unifies, not only the man and the woman as husband and wife, but also unifies families - the two families of origin of each of the couple and their extended families; and communities, which may sometimes imply ethnic groups. Some intertribal marriages have engendered peace between communities in some nations in times past.

(6) Helps in Parenting.

Parenting is an honest, complex and delicate task that involves caring, training/education, being a role model, person development, etc. Parenting is a great subject in Sociology and Psychology, and where only one parent alone does it, it becomes a terrible task to undertake. Secondly, every child needs traits of a mother and of a father in him or her, and when one is totally absent the child is incompletely made. Marriage, therefore, provides the natural basis for two to do parenting without any suspicion.[11]

(7) Place For Healthy Child Upbringing.

Marriage provides the platform for healthy bringing of children. When a husband and his wife bring up their child, the child sees his/her parents as such - no moral issues may arise. But when a single parent brings up a child, chances are that the parent's friends (men or women) - likely at different times - who do not really belong to the family. There are parents who have children from different members of the opposite sex - for example, a man having three children from three different women, not because the wives died, but due to promiscuity or divorces. Moral issues arise in such a situation. Note that children are faster in imbibing what they see than practicing what they are instructed.

(8) Maturity and Responsibility.

---

[11] Actions of a parent may at times be viewed with suspicion where one is a step-parent.

Marriage makes many people mature and more responsible. Whether at home or outside home, parents are supposed to be conscious of the fact that their children are listening and all are watching, hence control their actions. Secondly, parents who care for and about their child/children do not spend frivolously. They plan for now and the future. Each spouse also has in mind the partner while planning or executing plans. There's a remarkable difference between the driving style of a young unmarried person and that of a married person who always remembers that there is someone else of his or her responsibility that may be affected adversely by the outcome of any action taken.

(9) Marriage Typifies Jesus and The Church.[12]

Jesus Christ founded or built the church, which he said the gates of Hades or hell shall not overcome (Matthew 16:18 NIV). And Jesus loves the Church so much that He gave his life for it (John 15:13-14 "Greater love has no one than this, than to lay down one's life for his friends. [14] You are My friends if you do whatever I command you."

The church is described as the bride of Jesus Christ

---

[12] The Church is not a building in this context; it is Greek *ekklesia* = a gathering of believers in Jesus Christ (a.k.a. saints)

- her Groom (Revelation 21:9-11). It is necessary to study Ephesians 5:22-33:

"**22** Wives, submit to your own husbands, as to the Lord. **23** For the husband is head of the wife, as also Christ is head of the church; and He is the Savior of the body. **24** Therefore, just as the church is subject to Christ, so *let* the wives *be* to their own husbands in everything.

25 Husbands, love your wives, just as Christ also loved the church and gave Himself for her, **26** that He might sanctify and cleanse her with the washing of water by the word, **27** that He might present her to Himself a glorious church, not having spot or wrinkle or any such thing, but that she should be holy and without blemish. **28** So husbands ought to love their own wives as their own bodies; he who loves his wife loves himself. **29** For no one ever hated his own flesh, but nourishes and cherishes it, just as the Lord *does* the church. **30** For we are members of His body, of His flesh and of His bones. **31** "For this reason a man shall leave his father and mother and be joined to his wife, and the two shall become one flesh." **32** This is a great mystery, but I speak concerning Christ and the church. **33** Nevertheless let each one of you in particular so love his own wife as himself, and let the wife *see* that she respects *her* husband."

Proper marriage, where the wife respects her husband and the husband loves (Grk: *agapa*) his wife, typifies the marriage of Christ and his church. The church is totally subject to have Founder and Sustainer and at the end of the day He will take her to Himself. The marriage feast will take place - Revelations 19:6-9:

"And I heard, as it were, the voice of a great multitude, as the sound of many waters and as the sound of mighty thunderings, saying, "Alleluia! For the Lord God Omnipotent reigns! [7] Let us be glad and rejoice and give Him glory, for the marriage of the Lamb has come, and His wife has made herself ready." [8] And to her it was granted to be arrayed in fine linen, clean and bright, for the fine linen is the righteous acts of the saints.

[9] Then he said to me, "Write: 'Blessed *are* those who are called to the marriage supper of the Lamb!' " And he said to me, "These are the true sayings of God."

CHAPTER FIVE
MARRIAGE SUCCESS AND FAILURE

At what point do we grade a marriage successful? I once heard from my late father, never call a man successful until you see his end. This is also true of a marriage. For a marriage to be graded successful, at least the following should have happened or been present in the marriage: -

(a) It should be lifelong.

Marriage is meant to be for better for worse until death parts the couple. Jesus said in Matthew 19:6 NKJV "So then, they are no longer two but one flesh. Therefore what God has joined together, let not man separate." Also, Matthew 7: 39 - 40a. By the standards of God, no human being or institution is allowed to separate person s joined by God as husband and wife. This includ es the couple them selves. So, the marriage must have been character rized by the fear of God.

(b) the couple should have lived happily, each party see king to make the other happy.

(c) mutual respect should have characterized the marriage too, as that helps to keep away intruders.

(d) Mutual trust should also have been part of the marriage.

(e) "Behold, children are a gift of the Lord, The fruit of the womb is a reward." (Psalm 127:3 NASB). The blessing of children to a marriage is one of the marks of success of a marriage. It is God that gives children; if He gives the couple children, they should gladly welcome them and bring them up in the way and nurture of the Lord. Where God does not give biological children, the couple should not be regarded as failed because God might have a plan for them different from their thoughts. However, the marriage would have failed if the couple deliberately refused God-given children. This is because by refusing to bear children the couple has helped the devil in attempting to scuttle God's plan for humanity. Bearing children is not optional to a marriage except the will of God so dictates. I have met a man that always talked about his cat. When I asked, he said his wife did not want to bear children but was okay nurturing a cat.

(f) Proverbs 13:22 NKJV says, "A good *man* leaves an inheritance to his children's children, But the wealth of the sinner is stored up for the righteous."

An inheritance should be in the following forms colon

- Good training academically, morally, and religiously. Proverbs 22:6 says to train up a child in the way he should go and when he is old, he shall not depart from it.
- Financial wealth rather than debts;
- Material wealth including landed property and, all intellectual property. And inheritance constitutes a stepping stone for responsible or reasonable, well brought up children.

CHAPTER 6

MARRIAGE FAILURE

Simply put, failure is the opposite of success. It means falling short of an expected standard. The following, amongst others are causes and symptoms of a failing marriage: -

6.1 Causes and Symptoms of Marriage Failure

a) Poor communication is a principal cause of marriage failure. When one party often misunderstands the other and the misunderstood party does not patiently explain, problems begin to set him.

b) Unforgiveness leads to bitterness in any relationship. Everyone in any relationship is prone to offending another party in the relationship because no human being is perfect and no two persons like everything equally. One man's meet is said to be another's poison. Hence when one offends and the offended person fails to forgive it gradually adds up and builds up to bitterness.

c) Lack of togetherness why does the gap between a couple. When the couple do not create time to be together the gap between them begins to widen until the gap becomes a wall or gully.

d) Suspicion and secrecy - when one party suspects actions or utterances of the spouse or acts secretively, breakdown gradually sets in.

e) Disrespect. The male ego naturally demands respect, for which reason disrespect from the woman always breeds trouble. However, the wife also deserves respect and love, which compel the man to behave as *primus inter pares* (first among equals) in the home.

f) Lack of intimacy is both a cause and sign of failing marriage. The absence of intimacy is likely to drive the party deprived of it out to seek satisfaction outside.

g) Immorality/adultery is both causative and symptomatic of a failing marriage. It worsens the relationship between a man and his wife and could lead the immoral one's spouse to decide to go out too. It is often a sign of dissatisfaction in the sexual relationship in the home.

h) Feeling controlled buy one party breeds friction. Oftentimes it stems from pride and poor communication and inferiority complex.

i) Frequent threats of divorce is a sign of tiredness of the marriage.

j) Separation - where one party moves away from the house. The couple may live together under the same roof, go in and out separately and no longer cooperate for anything, though without a formal divorce. This is a major sign of marriage failure, which normally ends in divorce except there is divine intervention.

k) Lack of patience is a major cause of failure where one party or both act on impulse, without giving a second thought.

l) Pride often leads to a fall. When one party feels more advantaged than the other, or superior by any standard, there is bound to be friction.

m) Interference by third parties causes failure if the couple are unable to manage it. Interference may be by parents-in-law, brothers-, and sisters-in-law, friends or even professional service providers to the family.

n) Bad management of children – where one party pays more attention to the children than the spouse, that could lead to jealousy, and breakdown of law and order in the home.

o) Childlessness does cause or contribute to marriage failure, especially if the childlessness is self-inflicted.

6.2 Results of Marriage Failure.

The results of failure of a marriage vary from couple to couple, depending on the age of the marriage. They may include all or some of the following: -

i) Divorce of the couple marks the termination of the marriage. This is point of no return.

ii) Permanent enmity between the couple and the families on either side of the couple.

iii) No children between the couple either intentionally or due to tension and anxiety.

iv) Wayward children could be a result of failed or failing marriage, as the children become single-parent brought up, some of who have been seen to be deficient in the morals, some become street children with criminal tendencies.

v) Absence of sexual activities which could lead to frustration and immoral practices.

vi) It could cause some people to take consolation in hard drugs and/or alcohol, which are not without serious consequences or adverse outcomes. In extreme cases suicide or murder could result from failed marriage.

6.3 How to Save a Failing Marriage.

Every problem has a solution. Oftentimes the solution to your problem may tend to elude you due to ignorance, carelessness, pride or just lack of understanding. In Hosea 4:6 the Bible says that the Lord said, "My people are destroyed for lack of knowledge." The antidotes recommended hereunder are based on the symptoms listed in 6.1 above as follows: -

i. God is described as omnipotent; that is all-powerful at all times, omniscient - that is all-knowing, and omnipresent

(present in all places at the same time and at all times.) <u>God is also loving</u> -Romans 5:8 NASB "But God demonstrates His own love toward us, in that while we were still sinners, Christ died for us."

1 John 4:10 NASB "In this is love, not that we loved God, but that He loved us and sent His Son *to be* the propitiation for our sins."

<u>God is merciful</u> - Psalm 145:9 NASB "The Lord is good to all, And His mercies are over all His works."

<u>God is kind</u> –

Lamentations 3:33 NASB For He does not afflict Willingly Or grieve the sons of mankind."

<u>God is wise</u> –

Proverbs 3:19 NASB "The Lord founded the earth by wisdom,

He established the heavens by understanding."

And <u>God is just</u> - Luke 18:6-7 NASB "And the Lord said, "Listen to what the unrighteous judge said; [7] now, will God not bring about justice for His elect who cry out to Him day and night, and will He delay long for them?"

With these qualities of God, He is the greatest counselor, Judge and the Helper you can have. And as has been previously explained, God is the Author and Sustainer of marriage. Upon realizing that there is a problem in your marriage your first and best place or Person to go to for help is God in prayer.

Jesus said, "Come unto me all ye who labor and a heavy leading and I will give you rest." (Matthew 11:28). There are some other Bible passages that invite you to pray. Examples are:

"Casting all your care upon Him, for He cares for you." (1 Peter 5:7 NKJV).

"Be anxious for nothing, but in everything by prayer and supplication, with thanksgiving, let your requests be made known to God; [7] and the peace of God, which surpasses all understanding, will guard your hearts and minds through Christ Jesus." (Philippians 4:6-7 NKJV).

You do not need to pay any consultation fees to get to God. Access to Him is open 24/7. Tell God to forgive your sins and help you to overcome them. Ask Him to help you as you have no power of your own to achieve success and peace in your marriage.

ii. You have to depend on the Lord to help you in all matters. For every undertaking in your marriage, pray/ask and trust God to help you. Marriage is more of a spiritual matter, which cannot be successfully handled or approached physically.

iii. Marriage has principles in Scriptures, which if kept, have to promote healthiness of marriage. These principles should be followed where you have been failing. It is Ephesians 5:22-6:9 NASB:

"Wives, *subject yourselves* to your own husbands, as to the Lord. [23] For the husband is the head of the wife, as Christ also is the head of the church, He Himself *being* the Savior of the body. [24] But as the church is subject to Christ, so also the wives *ought to be* to their husbands in everything.

[25] Husbands, love your wives, just as Christ also loved the church and gave Himself up for her, [26] so that He might sanctify her, having cleansed her by the washing of water with the word, [27] that He might present to Himself the church in all her glory, having no spot or wrinkle or any such thing; but that she would be holy and blameless. [28] So husbands also ought to love their own wives as their own bodies. He who loves his own wife loves himself; [29] for no one ever hated his own flesh, but nourishes and cherishes it, just as Christ also *does* the church, [30] because we are parts of His body. [31] For this reason a man shall leave his father and his mother and be joined to his wife, and the two shall become one flesh. [32] This mystery is great; but I am speaking with reference to Christ and the church. [33] Nevertheless, as for you individually, each *husband* is to love his own wife the same as himself, and the wife *must see to it* that she respects her husband.

Children and Parents (Ephesians 6:1-3):

"Children, obey your parents in the Lord, for this is right. [2] Honor your father and mother (which is the first commandment with a promise), [3] so that it may turn out well for you, and that you may live long on the earth."

This passage speaks to wives, husbands, children of the husbands and wives, fathers, and masters and to servants in the home. Of course, the counsel to servants also applies to employees at workplace and the 'masters' as their employers. Let us read the passage thus:

Wives:

Ephesians 5:22-24, 33 NIV "Wives, submit yourselves to your own husbands as you do to the Lord. [23] For the husband is the head of the wife as Christ is the head of the church, his body, of which he is the Savior. [24] Now as the church submits to Christ, so also wives should submit to their husbands in everything."

[33] However, each one of you also must love his wife as he loves himself, and the wife must respect her husband.

Colossians 3:18 NIV "Wives, submit yourselves to your husbands, as is fitting in the Lord."

Husbands:

Ephesians 5: 25- 33 NIV "Husbands, love your wives, just as Christ loved the church and gave himself up for her [26] to make her holy, cleansing her by the washing with water through the word, ²⁷ and to present her to himself as a radiant church, without stain or wrinkle or any other blemish, but holy and blameless. ²⁸ In this same way, husbands ought to love their wives as their own bodies. He who loves his wife loves himself. ²⁹ After all, no one ever hated their own body, but they feed and care for their body, just as Christ does the church— ³⁰ for we are members of his body. ³¹ "For this reason a man will leave his father and mother and be united to his wife, and the two will become one flesh." ³² This is a profound mystery—but I am talking about Christ and the church. ³³ However, each one of you also must love his wife as he loves himself, and the wife must respect her husband."

Colossians 3: 19 NIV "Husbands, love your wives and do not be harsh with them."

Children:

Ephesians 6:1-3 NIV "Children, obey your parents in the Lord, for this is right. ² "Honor your father and mother"— which is the first commandment with a promise— ³ "so that it may go well with you and that you may enjoy long life on the earth."

Colossians 3:20 NIV "Children, obey your parents in everything, for this pleases the Lord."

Husbands as the fathers

Ephesians 6:4 NIV "Fathers, do not exasperate your children; instead, bring them up in the training and instruction of the Lord."

Colossians 3:21 NIV "Fathers, do not embitter your children, or they will become discouraged."

Servants:

Ephesians 6:5-8 NIV "Slaves, obey your earthly masters with respect and fear, and with sincerity of heart, just as you would obey Christ. [6] Obey them not only to win their favor when their eye is on you, but as slaves of Christ, doing the will of God from your heart. [7] Serve wholeheartedly, as if you were serving the Lord, not people, [8] because you know that the Lord will reward each one for whatever good they do, whether they are slave or free."

Colossians 3:22- 25 NIV "Slaves, obey your earthly masters with respect and fear, and with sincerity of heart, just as you would obey Christ. [6] Obey them not only to win their favor when their eye is on you, but as slaves of Christ, doing the will of God from your heart. [7] Serve wholeheartedly, as if you were serving the Lord, not people, [8] because you know that the Lord will reward each one for whatever good they do, whether they are slave or free."

Husbands as masters

Ephesians 6:9 NIV "And masters, treat your slaves in the same way. Do not threaten them, since you know that he who is both their Master and yours is in heaven, and there is no favoritism with him."

Colossians 4:1 NIV "Masters, provide your slaves with what is right and fair, because you know that you also have a Master in heaven."

iv. Resolve to love your spouse as Jesus loves you, and as He loves His Bride - the Church, to the extent of giving His life for her sake. Do this in reverence for God.

v. Humility is one of the fruit of the Holy Spirit found in Galatians 5:19 to 21. When your life is filled and controlled by the Holy Spirit, humility becomes one of your character traits. But you must be a child of God to invite the Holy Spirit into your life daily. The Apostle Paul said you should be filled with the Holy Spirit daily. He wrote Ephesians 5:18. To be filled with wine is a deliberate voluntary action, and it is simple. Rather, be or keep on being filled with the Holy spirit. Each time, ask Him to fill you up when. He fills you He empowers you to do spiritual things, including managing your spouse.

vi. You can then put your pride aside (swallow your pride) to take all the necessary steps to save your marriage, including overlooking insults from your spouse. Remember that pride goes before a fall.

vii. Initiate reconciliation between you and your spouse after asking God to direct you. God is the Author of peace; when you want peace between you and your spouse God will empower you to seek it. "Blessed are the peacemakers in bracket for they will be called children of God." (Matthew 5:9) Also the psalmist wrote, "Turn from evil and do   good; seek peace and pursue it." (Psalm 34:14 NIV). Also, Hebrews 12:14-16 NIV reads, "Make every effort to live in peace with everyone and to be holy; without holiness no one will see the Lord. [15] See to it that no one falls short of the grace of God and that no bitter root grows up to cause trouble and defile many. [16] See that no one is sexually immoral, or is godless like Esau, who for a single meal sold his inheritance rights as the oldest son."

viii. Make yourself available to your family. They need your company and attention. Give it to them.

ix. Respect your spouse - avoiding things he or she does not like and promote the things that he/she does like. Do remember that love is not just a feeling but an action. Love gives. Show love to your spouse. Recall old times when your spouse was darling and all nice things that he or she did for you.

x. Mind your language. Never allow threats of divorce or separation proceed from your mouth anymore. There is power in the word of mouth. Things (words and statements) you repeat do come to pass, and scripture says, "But I tell you that everyone will have to give account on the day of judgment for every empty word they have spoken." (Matthew 12:36 NIV).

CHAPTER SEVEN
BRIEF NOTES ON DIVORCE

Divorce has some implications on marriage, and in view of that and God's attitude towards it, it becomes necessary to discuss divorce in this chapter, howbeit briefly under the following headings: definition, statistics, causes and effects.

Webster's Dictionary defines divorce as "An act or instance of legally dissolving a marriage."[13] This implies putting away of one's spouse with the approval of a relevant institution, principality the court of law.

It has been gathered from "Marriage and Divorce" by the National Center for Health Statistics of Centers for Disease Control and Prevention (CDC)[14] that in 2021 there were 689,308 in forty-five states and DC in the USA - a rate of 2.5 per 1,000.

Studies have shown that a high percentage of couples that get involved in trial marriage - cohabiting before really formalizing the marriage - end up in divorce. And some

---

[13] Webster's All-in-One Dictionary & Thesaurus, 188.
[14] Centers for Disease Control and Prevention. "Marriage and Divorce." https://www.cdc.gov/nchs/fastats/marriage-divorce.htm

other common reasons for which couples divorce include the following: -

1) Lack of genuine commitment to making the marriage last long. There are a couple of factors that account for this including unbroken previous relationships, as well as not leaving and cleaving (and continually looking back to parental status especially if rich).

2) Immorality or infidelity on the part of one or both of the couple.

3) Domestic violence.

4) Unforgiveness by one of or both of the couple.

5) Substantial and unexpected increase in wealth may lead to desire of one party to divorce in order to split the wealth, although it is believed that the rate of divorce is higher among couples that are below poverty level. In effect lack also could lead to divorce. In effect, lack is also capable of leading a couple to divorce.

EFFECTS OF DIVORCE

A. On The Couple Themselves

Certainly, every divorce leaves many scars which may impact each of the erstwhile couple differently. Recall two scriptures: 1 Corinthians 6:16 NIV: "Do you not know that he who unites himself with a prostitute is one with her in body? For it is said, "The two will become one flesh." and Matthew 19:4-6 NIV: "Haven't you read," he replied, "that at the beginning the Creator 'made them male and female,' [5] and said, 'For this reason a man will leave his father and mother and be united to his wife, and the two will become one flesh'? [6] So they are no longer two, but one flesh. Therefore what God has joined together, let no one separate."

The meaning given to divorce appears or sounds too mild for what actually happens in most divorce instances. I would rather define divorce as *tearing apart a married couple,* as every tearing leaves behind some pain and scars, some of which may be irreparable damage. Some of such effects are listed as follows: -

    i. Decrease in levels of happiness.

    ii. Change in economic status - for the better or otherwise, depending on the reason for divorce.

    iii. Emotional and psychological problems which could usher in some health issues.

    iv. Increase in the risk of mortality.

    B. On Other People

Just like every marriage impacts other people including children (born or later brought into the marriage), families and friends of the couple, the church or community.

On The Children.

There are physical, emotional, and psychological effects on the children: -

1) Diminished trust in one of the parents especially the one that loses custody of the children.
2) Issues of Mental Health.
3) Psychological problems.
4) Behavioral problems – may include drug and alcohol.
5) Anger
6) Poor performance in academics
7) Unwanted pregnancy
8) Straying into gangs and cults
9) Lack of interest in, and disrespect for, marriage.

C. On Family And Community

The families and friends that were joined together by the marriage are also torn (ripped) apart, and relationships previously established get mostly terminated. This is because the marriage that previously constituted a bridge between them is now broken. Fellowship in the same church, where the couple belonged as members get a bit sour, as each party may have other members taking sides inevitably.

ISSUES THAT MUST BE ADDRESSED

(1) Child custody - by the Authority granting the divorce.

(2) Child support

(3) Alimony

(4) Property sharing

(5) Relocation of the divorcing spouses.

REMEDIES FOR DIVORCE

Just as it is important to prevent separation from occurring rather than mending it when it has already happened, it is better and somewhat easier to prevent a divorce than to begin to seek a solution sequel to its occurrence with accompanying regrets. Some ways to prevent divorce are as follows: -

i.   Fear Of God

The Bible says that God hates divorce. If you have the fear of God, you will avoid offending, or going against, God and His will. Similarly, we read that anyone who divorces his or her spouse and marries another commits adultery, which, like other sins is capable of earning the one a place in Hellfire. The fear of God is the beginning of wisdom.

ii. Counseling.

When the relationship begins to go sour, the couple should consider going to consult a marriage counselor for help - preferably a pastor that will include praying in his counseling program. Any other professional counselor maybe consulted where the couple are unbelievers.

iii. Pray and Talk About the Issues.

Jointly and individually pray to the Author of marriage concerning the state of your marriage and talk about the issues threatening the marriage. Each spouse should swallow their pride, humble themselves, be accountable. Be the first to initiate discussion of the issues. Throw away feelings of superiority over your spouse

iv. Remember, No Infallibility - No One Is Perfect.

You should remind yourself that as human, your spouse is not infallible. Do not expect too much from any human being - he or she is prone to errors like you. Both of you did not come out of the same womb, neither were you brought up in the same family. This implies that the background differences should be born in mind while seeking reconciliation.

v. Forgiveness.

Develop a forgiving heart. Jesus said, "For if you forgive other people when they sin against you, your heavenly Father will also forgive you. [15] But if you do not forgive others their sins, your Father will not forgive your sins."

(Matthew 6:14-15 NIV). Although Jesus confirmed that in the permissive will of God, adultery is the only grounds for divorce (Matthew 19:8) yet, He also taught that the only sin that is unforgivable is sin against the Holy Spirit. That is why to the question of Peter on how many times a brother may offend before he stops being forgiven, Jesus replied 70 x 7 times (Matthew 18:21-22). Do well to study a parable Jesus spoke on forgiveness in Matthew 18:21-35 NIV as follows:

"Then Peter came to Jesus and asked, "Lord, how many times shall I forgive my brother or sister who sins against me? Up to seven times?"

[22] Jesus answered, "I tell you, not seven times, but seventy-seven times. [23] "Therefore, the kingdom of heaven is like a king who wanted to settle accounts with his servants. [24] As he began the settlement, a man who owed him ten thousand bags of gold was brought to him. [25] Since he was not able to pay, the master ordered that he and his wife and his children and all that he had be sold to repay the debt. [26] "At this the servant fell on his knees before him. 'Be patient with me,' he begged, 'and I will pay back everything.' [27] The servant's master took pity on him, canceled the debt and let him go.

[28] "But when that servant went out, he found one of his fellow servants who owed him a hundred silver coins. He

grabbed him and began to choke him. 'Pay back what you owe me!' he demanded. [29] "His fellow servant fell to his knees and begged him, 'Be patient with me, and I will pay it back.' [30] "But he refused. Instead, he went off and had the man thrown into prison until he could pay the debt. [31] When the other servants saw what had happened, they were outraged and went and told their master everything that had happened.

[32] "Then the master called the servant in. 'You wicked servant,' he said, 'I canceled all that debt of yours because you begged me to. [33] Shouldn't you have had mercy on your fellow servant just as I had on you?' [34] In anger his master handed him over to the jailers to be tortured, until he should pay back all he owed. [35] "This is how my heavenly Father will treat each of you unless you forgive your brother or sister from your heart."

vi. Spend Time Together.

Each spouse must create time to be spent regularly with the other. Oftentimes, issues of sex - too much demand for it or too much refusal – lead to contemplation of divorce.

Remember 1Corinthians 7:5 NLT.: Do not deprive each other of sexual relations, unless you both agree to refrain from sexual intimacy for a limited time so you can give yourselves more completely to prayer. Afterward, you should come together again so that Satan won't be able to tempt you because of your lack of self-control."

BIBLE VERSES ON DIVORCE ("putting away" = Greek *apostasion*)

Deuteronomy 22:13-19; 29 NKJV "If any man takes a wife, and goes in to her, and detests her, [14] and charges her with shameful conduct, and brings a bad name on her, and says, 'I took this woman, and when I came to her I found she *was* not a virgin,' [15] then the father and mother of the young woman shall take and bring out *the evidence of* the young woman's virginity to the elders of the city at the gate. [16] And the young woman's father shall say to the elders, 'I gave my daughter to this man as wife, and he detests her. [17] Now he has charged her with shameful conduct, saying, "I found your daughter *was* not a virgin," and yet these *are the evidences of* my daughter's virginity.' And they shall spread the cloth before the elders of the city. [18] Then the elders of that city shall take that man and punish him; [19] and they shall fine him one hundred *shekels* of silver and give *them* to the father of the young woman, because he has brought a bad name on a virgin of Israel. And she shall be his wife; he cannot divorce her all his days.

²⁹ then the man who lay with her shall give to the young woman's father fifty *shekels* of silver, and she shall be his wife because he has humbled her; he shall not be permitted to divorce her all his days.

Deuteronomy 24:1-4 NASB "When a man takes a wife and marries her, and it happens, if she finds no favor in his eyes because he has found some indecency in her, that he writes her a certificate of divorce, puts *it* in her hand, and sends her away from his house, ² and she leaves his house and goes and becomes another man's *wife*, ³ and the latter husband turns against her, writes her a certificate of divorce and puts *it* in her hand, and sends her away from his house, or if the latter husband who took her to be his wife dies, ⁴ *then* her former husband who sent her away is not allowed to take her again to be his wife, after she has been defiled; for that is an abomination before the Lord, and you shall not bring sin on the land which the Lord your God is giving you as an inheritance."

Jeremiah 3:8 NASB "And I saw that for all the adulteries of faithless Israel, I had sent her away and given her a certificate of divorce, yet her treacherous sister Judah did not fear; but she went and prostituted herself also."

Ezekiel 44:22 NASB "And they shall not marry a widow or a divorced woman, but shall take virgins from the descendants of the house of Israel, or a widow who is the widow of a priest."

Malachi 2:15-16 NASB "But not one has done *so* who has a remnant of the Spirit. And why the one? He was seeking a godly offspring. Be careful then about your spirit, and *see that* none *of you* deals treacherously against the wife of your youth. [16] "For I hate divorce," says the Lord, the God of Israel, "and him who covers his garment with violence," says the Lord of armies. "So be careful about your spirit, that you do not deal treacherously."

Matthew 19:8-9 NASB "He said to them, "Because of your hardness of heart Moses permitted you to divorce your wives; but from the beginning it has not been this way. [9] And I say to you, whoever divorces his wife, except for sexual immorality, and marries another woman commits adultery.""

Mark 10:11-12 NASB "And He said to them, "Whoever divorces his wife and marries another woman commits adultery against her; [12] and if she herself divorces her husband and marries another man, she is committing adultery.""

Luke 16:18 NASB "Everyone who divorces his wife and marries another commits adultery, and he who marries one who is divorced from a husband commits adultery."

CHAPTER EIGHT

BIBLE PASSAGES ABOUT MARRIAGE.

Like many or, in fact, every other subject about life of human beings, the Bible has passages about, and should help, your marriage and related issues. Just as a reminder, or if you have never known it, the Bible is a "library" (a collection) of 66 books written by about 40 men inspired by the Holy Spirit of God, over a period of about 2,000 years, at various locations in the world. The books in the Bible are grouped into the Old Testament and the New Testament.

The Old Testament comprises 39 books from Genesis to Malachi, while the New Testament consists of 27 books - Matthew to Revelation.

The Apostle Paul wrote, "All Scripture is inspired by God and is useful to teach us what is true and to make us realize what is wrong in our lives. It corrects us when we are wrong and teaches us to do what is right. [17] God uses it to prepare and equip his people to do every good work." (2 Timothy 3:16-17 NLT). Also, the Apostle Peter wrote, "Above all, you must realize that no prophecy in Scripture ever came from the prophet's own understanding" (2 Peter 1:20 NLT).

In view of these, it is advisable to study the Bible (the Word of God), and do what it teaches. Below are some verses of scripture relevant to our subject – your marriage and related matters.

Genesis 1:28 "And God blessed them, and God said unto them, Be fruitful, and multiply, and replenish the earth, and subdue it: and have dominion over the fish of the sea, and over the fowl of the air, and over every living thing that moveth upon the earth."

Genesis 2:18-24 NKJV "And the Lord God said, "*It is* not good that man should be alone; I will make him a helper comparable to him." [19] Out of the ground the Lord God formed every beast of the field and every bird of the air, and brought *them* to Adam to see what he would call them. And whatever Adam called each living creature, that *was* its name. [20] So Adam gave names to all cattle, to the birds of the air, and to every beast of the field. But for Adam there was not found a helper comparable to him. [21] And the Lord God caused a deep sleep to fall on Adam, and he slept; and He took one of his ribs, and closed up the flesh in its place. [22] Then the rib which the Lord God had taken from man He made into a woman, and He brought her to the man. [23] And Adam said: "This *is* now bone of my bones And flesh of my flesh; She shall be called Woman,

Because she was taken out of Man." [24] Therefore a man shall leave his father and mother and be joined to his wife, and they shall become one flesh.

Deuteronomy 24:5 NKJV "When a man has taken a new wife, he shall not go out to war or be charged with any business; he shall be free at home one year, and bring happiness to his wife whom he has taken."
This is an extended honeymoon at which time the newly wed get used to each other and begin to get to know each other. This emphasizes the need for a newly married couple to stay together.

Ruth 1:16-17 NKJV "But Ruth said:
"Entreat me not to leave you, *Or to* turn back from following after you;
For wherever you go, I will go; And wherever you lodge, I will lodge;
Your people *shall be* my people, And your God, my God.
[17] Where you die, I will die, And there will I be buried.
The Lord do so to me, and more also, If *anything but* death parts you and me."
While these statements by Ruth to Naomi, her erstwhile mother-in-law were not instructions or a law related to marriage, they are the kind of strong vow that should

characterize a serious marriage. This accounts for the introduction of the statements in the traditional Christian wedding program.

Psalm 143:8 NKJV "Cause me to hear Your

lovingkindness in the morning,

For in You do I trust; Cause me to know the way in which I should walk, For I lift up my soul to You."

Psalm 127 NKJV "Unless the LORD builds the house, They labor in vain who build it;
Unless the LORD guards the city, The watchman stays awake in vain. [2] It is vain for you to rise up early, To sit up late, To eat the bread of sorrows; For so He gives His beloved sleep. [3] Behold, children are a heritage from the LORD, The fruit of the womb is a reward.
[4] Like arrows in the hand of a warrior, So are the children of one's youth. [5] Happy is the man who has his quiver full of them; They shall not be ashamed, But shall speak with their enemies in the gate."

Psalm 128: 1-2 NKJV "Blessed *is* every one who fears the Lord, Who walks in His ways.
[2] When you eat the labor of your hands, You *shall be* happy, and *it shall be* well with you."

Proverbs 5:16-20 NKJV "Should your fountains be dispersed abroad, Streams of water in the streets? [17] Let them be only your own, And not for strangers with you.

[18] Let your fountain be blessed, And rejoice with the wife of your youth. [19] *As a* loving deer and a graceful doe, Let her breasts satisfy you at all times; And always be enraptured with her love. [20] For why should you, my son, be enraptured by an immoral woman, And be embraced in the arms of a seductress?"

Proverbs 10:11-12 NKJV "The mouth of the righteous *is* a well of life,
But violence covers the mouth of the wicked. [12] Hatred stirs up strife, But love covers all sins."

Proverbs 16:3 NKJV "Commit your works to the Lord, And your thoughts will be established."

Proverbs 19:14 NKJV "Houses and riches *are* an inheritance from fathers, But a prudent wife *is* from the Lord."

Proverbs 12:4 NKJV "An excellent wife *is* the crown of her husband, But she who causes shame *is* like rottenness in his bones."

Proverbs 18:22 NKJV "*He who* finds a wife finds a good *thing,* And obtains favor from the Lord."

Ecclesiastes 4:9-12 NKJV "Two *are* better than one,

Because they have a good reward for their labor.

[10] For if they fall, one will lift up his companion.

But woe to him *who is* alone when he falls,

For *he has* no one to help him up.

[11] Again, if two lie down together, they will keep warm;

But how can one be warm *alone?*

[12] Though one may be overpowered by another, two can

withstand him.

And a threefold cord is not quickly broken."

Song of Solomon 8:6-7 NKJV "Set me as a seal upon your

heart,

As a seal upon your arm;

For love *is as* strong as death,

Jealousy *as* cruel as the grave;

Its flames *are* flames of fire,

A most vehement flame.

[7] Many waters cannot quench love,

Nor can the floods drown it.

If a man would give for love

All the wealth of his house,

It would be utterly despised."

Song of Solomon 2:16 NKJV "My beloved *is* mine, and
I *am* his.

He feeds *his flock* among the lilies."

Jeremiah 3:1 NLT "If a man divorces a woman and she
goes and marries someone else, he will not take her back
again, for that would surely corrupt the land. But you have
prostituted yourself with many lovers, so why are
you trying to come back to me?" says the Lord."

Malachi 2:14-16 NKJV "Yet you say, "For what reason?"
Because the Lord has been witness Between you and the
wife of your youth, With whom you have dealt
treacherously; Yet she is your companion And your wife by
covenant.
15 But did He not make *them* one, Having a remnant of the
Spirit?
And why one? He seeks godly offspring.
Therefore take heed to your spirit,
And let none deal treacherously with the wife of his youth.
16 "For the Lord God of Israel says That He hates divorce,
For it covers one's garment with violence," Says
the Lord of hosts.
"Therefore take heed to your spirit, That you do not deal
treacherously."

Matthew 5:21-22 NLT "You have heard that our ancestors were told, 'You must not murder. If you commit murder, you are subject to judgment.' ²² But I say, if you are even angry with someone, you are subject to judgment! If you call someone an idiot, you are in danger of being brought before the court. And if you curse someone, you are in danger of the fires of hell.

Matthew 5:27-28 NLT "You have heard the commandment that says, 'You must not commit adultery.' ²⁸ But I say, anyone who even looks at a woman with lust has already committed adultery with her in his heart."

Matthew 5:31-32 NLT "You have heard the law that says, 'A man can divorce his wife by merely giving her a written notice of divorce.' ³² But I say that a man who divorces his wife, unless she has been unfaithful, causes her to commit adultery. And anyone who marries a divorced woman also commits adultery."

Matthew 19:4-7 NLT "Haven't you read the Scriptures?" Jesus replied. "They record that from the beginning 'God made them male and female.'" ⁵ And he said, "'This explains why a man leaves his father and mother and is joined to his wife, and the two are united into one.' ⁶ Since they are no longer two but one, let no one split apart what God has joined together." ⁷ "Then why did Moses say in the law that a man could give his wife a written notice of divorce and send her away?" they asked."

Matthew 19:8-9 NLT "Jesus replied, "Moses permitted divorce only as a concession to your hard hearts, but it was not what God had originally intended. ⁹ And I tell you this, whoever divorces his wife and marries someone else commits adultery—unless his wife has been unfaithful."

Mark 10:2-12 NLT "Some Pharisees came and tried to trap him with this question: "Should a man be allowed to divorce his wife?" ³ Jesus answered them with a question: "What did Moses say in the law about divorce?" ⁴ "Well, he permitted it," they replied. "He said a man can give his wife a written notice of divorce and send her away."
⁵ But Jesus responded, "He wrote this commandment only as a concession to your hard hearts. ⁶ But 'God made them male and female' from the beginning of creation. ⁷ 'This explains why a man leaves his father and mother and is joined to his wife, ⁸ and the two are united into one.' Since they are no longer two but one, ⁹ let no one split apart what God has joined together."

¹⁰ Later, when he was alone with his disciples in the house, they brought up the subject again. ¹¹ He told them, "Whoever divorces his wife and marries someone else commits adultery against her. ¹² And if a woman divorces her husband and marries someone else, she commits adultery."

Luke 16:17-18 NLT "But that doesn't mean that the law has lost its force. It is easier for heaven and earth to disappear than for the smallest point of God's law to be overturned. ¹⁸ "For example, a man who divorces his wife and marries someone else commits adultery. And anyone who marries a woman divorced from her husband commits adultery."

John 2:1-11 NLT "The next day there was a wedding celebration in the village of Cana in Galilee. Jesus' mother was there, ² and Jesus and his disciples were also invited to the celebration. ³ The wine supply ran out during the festivities, so Jesus' mother told him, "They have no more wine."
⁴ "Dear woman, that's not our problem," Jesus replied. "My time has not yet come."
⁵ But his mother told the servants, "Do whatever he tells you."

⁶ Standing nearby were six stone water jars, used for Jewish ceremonial washing. Each could hold twenty to thirty gallons. ⁷ Jesus told the servants, "Fill the jars with water." When the jars had been filled, ⁸ he said, "Now dip some out, and take it to the master of ceremonies." So the servants followed his instructions. ⁹ When the master of ceremonies tasted the water that was now wine, not knowing where it had come from (though, of course, the servants knew), he called the bridegroom over. ¹⁰ "A host always serves the best wine first," he said. "Then, when everyone has had a lot to drink, he brings out the less expensive wine. But you have kept the best until now!" ¹¹ This miraculous sign at Cana in Galilee was the first time Jesus revealed his glory. And his disciples believed in him."

John 13:34-35 NLT "So now I am giving you a new commandment: Love each other. Just as I have loved you, you should love each other. ³⁵ Your love for one another will prove to the world that you are my disciples."

John 15:12-13 NLT "This is my commandment: Love each other in the same way I have loved you. ¹³ There is no greater love than to lay down one's life for one's friends."

Romans 7:2-3 NLT "For example, when a woman marries, the law binds her to her husband as long as he is alive. But if he dies, the laws of marriage no longer apply to her. [3] So while her husband is alive, she would be committing adultery if she married another man. But if her husband dies, she is free from that law and does not commit adultery when she remarries."

Romans 12:12 NLT "Rejoice in our confident hope. Be patient in trouble, and keep on praying."

Romans 13:8 NLT "Owe nothing to anyone—except for your obligation to love one another. If you love your neighbor, you will fulfill the requirements of God's law."

1 Corinthians 7:2-5 NLT "But because there is so much sexual immorality, each man should have his own wife, and each woman should have her own husband. [3] The husband should fulfill his wife's sexual needs, and the wife should fulfill her husband's needs. [4] The wife gives authority over her body to her husband, and the husband gives authority over his body to his wife. [5] Do not deprive each other of sexual relations, unless you both agree to refrain from sexual intimacy for a limited time so you can give yourselves more completely to prayer. Afterward, you

should come together again so that Satan won't be able to tempt you because of your lack of self-control."

1 Corinthians 7:10-13 NLT "But for those who are married, I have a command that comes not from me, but from the Lord. A wife must not leave her husband. [11] But if she does leave him, let her remain single or else be reconciled to him. And the husband must not leave his wife. [12] Now, I will speak to the rest of you, though I do not have a direct command from the Lord. If a fellow believer has a wife who is not a believer and she is willing to continue living with him, he must not leave her. [13] And if a believing woman has a husband who is not a believer and he is willing to continue living with her, she must not leave him."

1 Corinthians 16:14 NLT "And do everything with love."

1 Corinthians 13:4-8 NLT "Love is patient and kind. Love is not jealous or boastful or proud [5] or rude. It does not demand its own way. It is not irritable, and it keeps no record of being wronged. [6] It does not rejoice about injustice but rejoices whenever the truth wins out. [7] Love never gives up, never loses faith, is always hopeful, and endures through every circumstance. [8] Prophecy and

speaking in unknown languages and special knowledge will become useless. But love will last forever!"

2 Corinthians 6:14-17 NLT "Do not be unequally yoked together with unbelievers. For what fellowship has righteousness with lawlessness? And what communion has light with darkness? [15] And what accord has Christ with Belial? Or what part has a believer with an unbeliever? [16] And what agreement has the temple of God with idols? For you are the temple of the living God. As God has said:
"I will dwell in them And walk among *them.* I will be their God, And they shall be My people." [17] Therefore "Come out from among them And be separate, says the Lord.
Do not touch what is unclean, And I will receive you."

Galatians 6:8-9 NKJV "For he who sows to his flesh will of the flesh reap corruption, but he who sows to the Spirit will of the Spirit reap everlasting life. [9] And let us not grow weary while doing good, for in due season we shall reap if we do not lose heart."

Ephesians 4:1-3, 32 NKJV "I, therefore, the prisoner of the Lord, beseech you to walk worthy of the calling with which you were called, [2] with all lowliness and gentleness, with longsuffering, bearing with one another in love, [3] endeavoring to keep the unity of the Spirit in the bond of peace. ³² And be kind to one another, tenderhearted, forgiving one another, even as God in Christ forgave you."

Ephesians 5:22-27 NKJV "Wives, submit to your own husbands, as to the Lord. ²³ For the husband is head of the wife, as also Christ is head of the church; and He is the Savior of the body. ²⁴ Therefore, just as the church is subject to Christ, so *let* the wives *be* to their own husbands in everything.
²⁵ Husbands, love your wives, just as Christ also loved the church and gave Himself for her, ²⁶ that He might sanctify and cleanse her with the washing of water by the word, ²⁷ that He might present her to Himself a glorious church, not having spot or wrinkle or any such thing, but that she should be holy and without blemish."

Ephesians 5:33 NKJV "Nevertheless let each one of you in particular so love his own wife as himself, and let the wife *see* that she respects *her* husband."

Philippians 4:4-9, 13 NKJV "Rejoice in the Lord always. Again I will say, rejoice!
⁵ Let your gentleness be known to all men. The Lord *is* at hand. ⁶ Be anxious for nothing, but in everything by prayer

and supplication, with thanksgiving, let your requests be made known to God; [7] and the peace of God, which surpasses all understanding, will guard your hearts and minds through Christ Jesus.

[8] Finally, brethren, whatever things are true, whatever things *are* noble, whatever things *are* just, whatever things *are* pure, whatever things *are* lovely, whatever things *are* of good report, if *there is* any virtue and if *there is* anything praiseworthy—meditate on these things. [9] The things which you learned and received and heard and saw in me, these do, and the God of peace will be with you. [13] I can do all things through Christ who strengthens me."

Colossians 3:14-19 NKJV "But above all these things put on love, which is the bond of perfection. [15] And let the peace of God rule in your hearts, to which also you were called in one body; and be thankful. [16] Let the word of Christ dwell in you richly in all wisdom, teaching and admonishing one another in psalms and hymns and spiritual songs, singing with grace in your hearts to the Lord. [17] And whatever you do in word or deed, *do* all in the name of the Lord Jesus, giving thanks to God the Father through Him.

[18] Wives, submit to your own husbands, as is fitting in the Lord.

[19] Husbands, love your wives and do not be bitter toward them."

Hebrews 13:4 NLT "Give honor to marriage, and remain faithful to one another in marriage. God will surely judge people who are immoral and those who commit adultery."

James 1:19-20 NLT "Understand this, my dear brothers and sisters: You must all be quick to listen, slow to speak, and slow to get angry. [20] Human anger does not produce the righteousness God desires."

1 Peter 3:1-7 NLT "In the same way, you wives must accept the authority of your husbands. Then, even if some refuse to obey the Good News, your godly lives will speak to them without any words. They will be won over [2] by observing your pure and reverent lives. [3] Don't be concerned about the outward beauty of fancy hairstyles, expensive jewelry, or beautiful clothes. [4] You should clothe yourselves instead with the beauty that comes from within, the unfading beauty of a gentle and quiet spirit, which is so precious to God. [5] This is how the holy women of old made themselves beautiful. They put their trust in God and accepted the authority of their husbands. [6] For instance, Sarah obeyed her husband, Abraham, and called him her

master. You are her daughters when you do what is right without fear of what your husbands might do.

[7] In the same way, you husbands must give honor to your wives. Treat your wife with understanding as you live together. She may be weaker than you are, but she is your equal partner in God's gift of new life. Treat her as you should so your prayers will not be hindered."

1 Peter 4:8 NLT "Most important of all, continue to show deep love for each other, for love covers a multitude of sins.

1 John 4:7-8 NLT "Dear friends, let us continue to love one another, for love comes from God. Anyone who loves is a child of God and knows God. [8] But anyone who does not love does not know God, for God is love."

1 John 4:12 NKJV "No one has seen God at any time. If we love one another, God abides in us, and His love has been perfected in us. [19] We love Him because He first loved us."

1 John 4:11-19 NKJV "Beloved, if God so loved us, we also ought to love one another.

[12] No one has seen God at any time. If we love one another, God abides in us, and His love has been perfected in

us. ¹³ By this we know that we abide in Him, and He in us, because He has given us of His Spirit. ¹⁴ And we have seen and testify that the Father has sent the Son *as* Savior of the world. ¹⁵ Whoever confesses that Jesus is the Son of God, God abides in him, and he in God. ¹⁶ And we have known and believed the love that God has for us. God is love, and he who abides in love abides in God, and God in him. ¹⁷ Love has been perfected among us in this: that we may have boldness in the day of judgment; because as He is, so are we in this world. ¹⁸ There is no fear in love; but perfect love casts out fear, because fear involves torment. But he who fears has not been made perfect in love. ¹⁹ We love Him because He first loved us."

Revelation 19:7-9 NKJV "Let us be glad and rejoice and give Him glory, for the marriage of the Lamb has come, and His wife has made herself ready." ⁸ And to her it was granted to be arrayed in fine linen, clean and bright, for the fine linen is the righteous acts of the saints. ⁹ Then he said to me, "Write: 'Blessed *are* those who are called to the marriage supper of the Lamb!' " And he said to me, "These are the true sayings of God."

CHAPTER NINE

THE MARRIAGE SUPPER OF THE LAMB.

The Marriage Supper of the Lamb is one of the events prop hesied to take place in the last days. This shall be the final Marriage which the angel in heaven announced is to take place as per Revelation 19:7 NLT: "Let us be glad and rejoice, and let us give honor to him. For the time has come f or the wedding feast of the Lamb, and his bride has prepared herself." The marriage shall be the demystification of the marriage of Christ and his Church mentioned by Paul the Apostle in Ephesians 5:31-32 NLT: ("As the Scriptures say, "A man leaves his father and mother and is joined to his wife, and the two are united into one." [32] This is a great mystery, but it is an illustration of the way Christ and the church are one."), which is represented or typified by the marriage of a man and a woman here on Earth.

The Marriage for which there shall be this Supper (Feast) shall be between Jesus Christ the Lamb of God and His Church. The church, as we noted earlier, is the gathering of believers in Christ - resurrected and *raptured* as we find in want 1Thessalonians 4:14-17 NLT which reads as follows:

"For since we believe that Jesus died and was raised to life again, we also believe that when Jesus returns, God will bring back with him the believers who have died.

[15] We tell you this directly from the Lord: We who are still living when the Lord returns will not meet him ahead of those who have died. [16] For the Lord himself will come down from heaven with a commanding shout, with the voice of the archangel, and with the trumpet call of God. First, the believers who have died will rise from their graves. [17] Then, together with them, we who are still alive and remain on the earth will be caught up in the clouds to meet the Lord in the air. Then we will be with the Lord forever."

Verse 17 is very relevant in this description of the church. At this point, Jesus Christ shall be reuniting with the church for whom He gave His life as a show of His love. 1Corinthians 15:51-53 NLT reads, "But let me reveal to you a wonderful secret. We will not all die, but we will all be transformed! [52] It will happen in a moment, in the blink of an eye, when the last trumpet is blown. For when the trumpet sounds, those who have died will be raised to live forever. And we who are living will also be transformed. [53] For our dying bodies must be transformed into bodies that will never die; our mortal bodies must be transformed into immortal bodies."

In effect the marriage is not going to include persons living on Earth. Let us read Revelation 19:5-9 NLT: "And from the throne came a voice that said, "Praise our God, all his servants, all who fear him, from the least to the greatest."

[6] Then I heard again what sounded like the shout of a vast crowd or the roar of mighty ocean waves or the crash of loud thunder: "Praise the Lord! For the Lord our God, the Almighty, reigns. [7] Let us be glad and rejoice, and let us give honor to him. For the time has come for the wedding feast of the Lamb, and his bride has prepared herself. [8] She has been given the finest of pure white linen to wear." For the fine linen represents the good deeds of God's holy people. [9] And the angel said to me, "Write this: Blessed are those who are invited to the wedding feast of the Lamb." And he added, "These are true words that come from God."

It is not explicitly stated when the Supper will take place, but it is inferable that it should be after the Rapture and before Christ's second coming to start his Millennial Kingdom. It is noteworthy that there will be joy in heaven when the Feast takes place. God will be praised and glorified as we read in Revelation 19:5-7 (reproduced above). The bride shall be dressed in clean and white fine linen which represents the righteous acts of the Bride (the saints) on Earth.

In Jesus' parable of the Marriage Feast recorded in Matthew 22:2-14, we see that everyone to be present at the Feast must appear in the right apparel - which this time is righteous acts, which are based on the righteousness of the Lamb of God, imputed on them.

The principal qualification of them that constitute the Bride is that they must all be born again to be addressed as saints. [15] The benefit of participating in this Marriage Supper of the Lamb as stated in Revelation 19:9 is that everyone INVITED (called) shall be called blessed.[16] But on the contrary the cost of missing the banquet shall be anything but blessed - Revelation 19:9 says: "And the angel said to me, "Write this: Blessed are those who are invited to

---

[15] *Practical Word Studies in the New Testament Vol. 2 L-Z* (page 1784) defines a saint as "a holy person, is a follower of the Lord Jesus Christ who has been set apart to live for God. The saint has given himself to live a consecrated, sacred, and holy life – all for the glory of God."
Some Bible verses at which living Christians are referred to as saints include Philippians 4:21-22 NKJV – "Greet every saint in Christ Jesus. The brethren who are with me greet you. [22] All the saints greet you, but especially those who are of Caesar's household."
Also, Colossians 1:1-2 NKJV – "**1** Paul, an apostle of Jesus Christ by the will of God, and Timothy our brother, [2] To the saints and faithful brethren in Christ *who are* in Colosse:
Grace to you and peace from God our Father and the Lord Jesus Christ."

[16] "Blessed are" (Greek: Μακάριοι (*Makarioi*)) translates to "Happy, blessed, to be envied."

the wedding feast of the Lamb." And he added, "These are true words that come from God."

The opposite of being blessed is being cursed, or disfavored - and should perish. In John 3:16 Jesus says, "For God so loved the world that He gave His only begotten Son, that whoever believes in Him should not perish but have everlasting life." The converse of this is also true: whoever does not believe should perish and not have eternal life.

To be qualified to be invited to the Marriage Supper of the Lamb, you must be born again. Jesus said to Nicodemus, "Truly, truly, I say to you, unless someone is born again he cannot see the kingdom of God." (John 3:3 NASB). When born again you become saved. In a similar manner, the Apostle Paul stated as per Romans 10: 9-11, "that if you confess with your mouth Jesus *as* Lord, and believe in your heart that God raised Him from the dead, you will be saved; [10] for with the heart *a person* believes, resulting in righteousness, and with the mouth he confesses, resulting in salvation. [11] For the Scripture says, "Whoever believes in Him will not be put to shame."

The implication of these is that it is in this life that you choose (and prepare) to be part of the Church – the Bride of the Lamb - and to partake of the Supper. Make efforts to prepare yourself daily for the Lord's coming. You must not miss the Marriage Supper of the Lamb.

Read the parable of the 10 virgins as follows in Matthew 25:1-13 NASB:

"Then the kingdom of heaven will be comparable to ten virgins, who took their lamps and went out to meet the groom. ² Five of them were foolish, and five were prudent. ³ For when the foolish took their lamps, they did not take *extra* oil with them; ⁴ but the prudent ones took oil in flasks with their lamps. ⁵ Now while the groom was delaying, they all became drowsy and *began* to sleep. ⁶ But at midnight there finally was a shout: 'Behold, the groom! Come out to meet *him*.' ⁷ Then all those virgins got up and trimmed their lamps. ⁸But the fooli sh *virgins* said to the prudent ones, 'Give us some of your oil, because our lamps are going out.' ⁹ However, the prudent ones answered, '*No*, there most certainly would not be enough for us and you *too*; go instead to the mer- chants and buy *some* for yourselves.' ¹⁰ But while they were on their way to buy *the oil*, the groom came, and those who were ready went in with him to the wedding feast; and the door was shut. ¹¹ Yet later, the other virgins also came, saying, 'Lord, lord, open up for us.' ¹² But he answered, 'Truly I say to you, I do not know you.' ¹³ Be on the alert then, because you do not know the day nor the hour."

Live everyday as if it were your last day. Keep your house in order always because you do not know when either Jesus will come and take His own people, or when death will knock on your door – and you cannot answer, 'come back later' or 'No'.

CHAPTER TEN
CONCLUSIONS AND RECOMMENDATIONS.

Marriage is the first institution in human history, having been created and ordained by the Almighty God, Creator of Heaven and Earth and all things and people in them. If God had not created or formed the woman for the man, probably bestiality would have been the order of the day. In effect God's creation of the woman as "a help meet fit for the [man]" brought completeness to the man and to humanity. So, a man is incomplete until he is married to the woman of God's choice for him. The same applies to the woman. In Proverbs 18:22 the Scripture says he who finds a wife finds a good thing and obtains favor from the Lord.

The verse does not say he who finds a woman because there is a difference between a wife and just any woman. While every wife is a woman, not every woman is a wife. A wife is a woman that unconditionally submits to her husband, and helps him, and respects him notwithstanding any form of superiority in their realities of life (say in income or financial background). Similarly, not all men are husbands; but all husbands are men. A husband is a man who genuinely loves his wife, in spite of any personal weaknesses she may have, like Jesus Christ loves His

Church to the extent of sacrificing His life for her. A husband cares and provides for his wife and entire family. And a loving husband also helps his wife in spite of her weaknesses or her strengths.

When a husband and his wife stay together and perform their roles accordingly the Author of marriage is glorified, as there is peace in the family as He designed it to be. "The family that prays together lives or stays together." As many marriages fail these days, many others succeed. This year 2023, a former president of the United States, Jimmy Carter is 98 years old having been born on October 1, 1924, and his wife by name Elena Rosalyn Carter is 95 years old (born on August 18th, 1927). Both of them have been married for 77 years since 1946 and they are still married and living together. I remember telling someone in 2021 that my wife and I were grateful to God for our 43rd wedding anniversary and he asked me in amazement, married to the same woman?

As the One that created the institution is ever present and concerned about the well-being of your marriage, trust in Him at every step and at all times in your marriage. Proverbs 3:5-6 NKJV says, "Trust in the Lord with all your heart, And lean not on your own understanding; [6] In all your ways acknowledge Him, And He shall direct your paths."

Take every misunderstanding to Him in prayer; take to Him Thanksgiving for every cause for rejoicing. A novel I read in my early high school years titled *The Thirty-Nine Steps* by John Buchan, published in 1915 by William Blackwood and sons, had as it's principal character Richard Hannay. If I am not mistaken, the main thing I remember in the book is Richard Hannay's statement that *"The secret of playing a part is to think yourself into it."* Resolve to make your marriage succeed for as long as you both shall live. Since it is "not by might nor by power, but by My Spirit says the Lord," depend on the Lord for wisdom, patience, and wherewith to make you a successful husband or wife. When you allow the fear, that is reverence or respect, of God to pervade your marriage He will help you. Study the manual for living - the Word of God - regularly (together and individually), and you will discover a lot of secrets that nobody might have told you.

The Bible is the book of which the Author, that is the Holy Spirit of God, is present when you read it. Get a copy today and begin to study it. I recommend you study closely the Apostle Paul's admonition to the church at Colosse. Though it was to the Church - the Bride of Christ - the message is applicable to a family that desires to stand the test of time (Colossians 3: 1-4:2).

Also take time off to read the marriage vows you said at your wedding, but if you did not do a wedding, plan one. However, it is important to note that for the Holy Spirit to be active in your life you must deliberately invite into your heart Jesus Christ, to be your Savior and Lord. Then you can love as He loves, and boldly depend on Him. You cannot depend on someone you do not know or have a relationship with. Stop what you are doing right now and offer a quick prayer as follows: "Lord Jesus, I confess that I am a sinner. Please forgive me of every sin in my life. Come to my heart as my Savior and Lord. I yield my life to you to control and use for your glory. Come into my marriage, stabilize and prosper it for your glory. I pray in your name. Amen."

If you are still single, I pray that the Lord will lead you to find His choice of life partner for you and may you live long and enjoy a successful married life. But if you are married and have some turbulence, I pray the Lord, the Prince of Peace to speak peace to the marriage right now. Amen. May the Lord help you as you get ready to partake of the Marriage Supper of the Lamb.

Jesus Christ is Lord! Hallelujah!

BIBLIOGRAPHY

Gromacki, Robert G. NEW TESTAMENT SURVEY. (Grand Rapids, MI: Baker
> Academic), 1974.

Inrig, Gary. GOD'S MYSTERIOUS WAYS. Suffering, Grace, and God's plan for
> Joseph. (Grand Rapids: Discovery House), 2016

Macarthur, John. THE GOSPEL ACCORDING TO JESUS: WHAT IS AUTHENTIC
> FAITH? (Grand Rapids, MI: Zondervan), 1988.

Walvoord, John F. THE RAPTURE QUESTION. (Grand Rapids: Zondervan Publishing
> House), 1979

Walvoord, John F. and Roy B. Zuck. THE BIBLE KNOWLEDGE COMMENTARY:
> EPISTLES & PROPHECY. (Colorado Springs: David C. Cook), 2018.

Willmington, H. L. WILLMINGTON'S GUIDE TO THE BIBLE. (Wheaton, Ill: Tyndale
> House Publishers. INC.), 1981

Worthington Jr. Everett L. (ed.). CHRISTIAN MARITAL COUNSELING: Eight
> Approaches to Helping Couples. (Eugene OR: Wipf and Stock Publishers), 1996.

Wright, H. Norman. THE PREMARITAL COUNSELING
HANDBOOK. (Chicago:

Moody Press), 1977, 1981, 1992.

Zuck, Roy B., Ed. A BIBLICAL THEOLOGY OF THE
NEW TESTAMENT. (Chicago:

Moody Press), 1994

LIFE APPLICATION STUDY BIBLE (NIV). (Carol
Stream, Ill: Tyndale House

Publishers, Inc.), 1992.

THE PASTOR'S HANDBOOK, Revised KJV Ed.
(Chicago, IL: Wing Spread

Publishers, 2003),

Scofield, C. I. (Ed.) THE HOLY BIBLE – AUTHORIZED
KING JAMES VERSION.

(New York: Oxford University Press), 1937

Practical Word Studies in the New Testament Vol. 2 L-Z

Webster's All-in-One Dictionary & Thesaurus.

National Center for Health Statistics

https://www.cdc.gov/nchs/fastats/marriage-divorce.htm

EDITOR'S REVIEW OF THE BOOK: GOD IS INTERESTED IN YOUR MARRIAGE:

Path to a Successful, Happy Christian Marriage

God Is Interested in Your Marriage: Path to a Successful, Happy Christian Marriage by Rev. Daniel U. Nwaelene, ThD., is one of those rare works that manages to be both timeless in its theology and timely in its application. From the very first page, the reader senses that this is not merely a book about marriage, but a pastoral voice calling Christians back to the heart of God's design for human relationships. Every sentence reflects the author's conviction that marriage was instituted by God, and that its flourishing is inseparable from His presence. Rather than offering quick fixes or cultural platitudes, the book is saturated with Scripture and prayerful wisdom, inviting readers to place their marriages on the solid foundation of God's Word.

What sets this work apart is its uncompromising grounding in Scripture. Instead of simply referencing verses, Rev. Nwaelene provides full quotations across multiple translations, KJV, NKJV, NASB, NIV, ESV, among others, ensuring that the Word itself stands front and center. This approach demonstrates both pastoral care and theological confidence: readers are not expected to pause, flip pages, or rely on half-remembered references. They are confronted directly with God's own words, raw and unfiltered, and then guided in their application to the realities of marriage. The result is a text that is not just instructional but devotional, encouraging readers to meditate on God's design as they learn.

The scope of the book is another of its great strengths. It is not written only for newlyweds or for couples in crisis, though both groups will find immense value within its pages. Instead, it is crafted for a wide spectrum of readers: singles discerning a future partner, engaged couples preparing for a covenantal union, married couples seeking to deepen their intimacy, divorced individuals longing for healing and clarity, and even pastors, parents, teachers, and marriage counselors. By casting its net so wide, the book refuses to pigeonhole marriage into a single

stage of life, instead treating it as a universal calling that touches families, communities, and the very witness of the Church.

Among the most striking sections are those dealing with the causes of marriage failure and the remedies available in Christ. Rev. Nwaelene speaks with honesty about the destructive effects of poor communication, unforgiveness, disrespect, adultery, pride, and secrecy. Yet he refuses to leave the reader in despair. Again and again he points toward prayer, humility, reconciliation, and the supernatural power of forgiveness as the pathways to renewal. His assertion that Jesus can "resurrect a dead marriage" echoes the gospel itself, reminding readers that no relationship is beyond the reach of God's redemptive hand. This is not a cold diagnosis but a compassionate invitation to trust the One who raised the dead to life.

The treatment of divorce is particularly noteworthy. While many contemporary voices either trivialize divorce or weaponize it, this book manages to navigate a faithful middle path. Rev. Nwaelene is uncompromising in affirming that God hates divorce, quoting Malachi and Jesus' words in the Gospels. Yet his tone is never harsh or judgmental. Instead, he approaches the subject with pastoral gravity, acknowledging its prevalence and its devastating consequences for spouses, children, and communities, while at the same time urging couples to exhaust every avenue of reconciliation before parting ways. He offers statistics, biblical reflection, and practical remedies, ensuring that this chapter speaks both to the mind and the heart.

At its theological core, the book insists on something that has been too often forgotten: marriage is not just a social contract or a human convenience. It is a living picture of Christ's covenant with His Church. In quoting Ephesians 5 and Revelation 19, Rev. Nwaelene reminds readers that marriage has eternal significance. Husbands are called to love sacrificially as Christ loved the Church, and wives to respect and honor as the Church responds to her Lord. This vision elevates the union of man and woman beyond companionship into a testimony of the gospel itself. It is this eschatological horizon, the vision of the Marriage Supper of the Lamb, that gives the entire book its urgency and its beauty.

Structurally, the book flows with admirable clarity. Beginning with the definition of marriage, moving through its divine origin, outlining its importance, and contrasting success with failure, the author builds his case step by step. The logical order

Makes it a valuable study guide for marriage preparation classes, a resource for pastors leading counseling sessions, or even a devotional tool for couples to work through together chapter by chapter. Each section is comprehensive yet digestible, and the progression from earthly marriage to the ultimate heavenly marriage provides the book with both narrative and theological unity.

The writing style deserves its own recognition. Rev. Nwaelene writes with a pastor's heart and a teacher's discipline. His sentences are clear and accessible, designed to reach believers of all backgrounds. He avoids needless academic jargon, but his respect for theological truth is evident on every page. Repetition is used skillfully: key truths such as "God is the Author of marriage," "God hates divorce," and "husbands must love, wives must respect" recur frequently, embedding themselves in the reader's memory. This repetition is not redundant; it is formative, reinforcing principles until they become convictions. His use of practical illustrations, such as the story of a woman marrying at sixty-eight or the critique of cohabitation as a poor substitute for covenant, grounds theological truths in everyday realities.

Technically, there are moments where the prose could be tightened. Some sentences are longer than necessary, and a handful of phrases reflect more oral preaching style than written polish. Yet these are minor quibbles that do not obscure meaning. If anything, they reveal the authenticity of a pastoral voice speaking directly to his people. And while the book could occasionally benefit from more explicit engagement with modern marital challenges, such as technology, social media pressures, or economic shifts, it remains solidly timeless in its principles. The truths it proclaims are as relevant today as they were in the days of Paul or Moses.

In the end, what emerges from this book is not just a manual on marriage but a testimony to God's faithfulness. Readers will walk away convinced that God cares deeply about their relationships, that His Word speaks directly to their struggles, and that with Him at the center, marriage can be not only enduring but joyful. For couples seeking healing, pastors searching for a reliable teaching resource, or young people preparing for lifelong commitment, this book offers both inspiration and instruction. It is a work that should find its place not only on personal bookshelves but also in church libraries, premarital classes, and counseling rooms.

God Is Interested in Your Marriage is ultimately a call to trust God with the most intimate covenant of human life. It is rich in Scripture, compassionate in tone, and prophetic in challenge. It deserves to be read widely, studied carefully, and most importantly, lived out faithfully. Rev. Nwaelene has given the Church not just another book on marriage, but a timeless guide that will remain relevant for generations to come.

Verdict: God Is Interested in Your Marriage is not just a book to read; it is a book to live by. It deserves a wide audience in churches, counseling offices, and Christian homes worldwide.

This book is a treasure for the Christian home. Its unwavering insistence that God, not psychology, culture, or personal opinion, is the foundation of marriage sets it apart from many modern guides. It is scripturally rich, pastorally compassionate, and theologically profound.

For married couples, it offers hope and tools for renewal. For pastors and counselors, it serves as a ready-made manual for premarital classes or crisis counseling. For the wider Church, it is a much-needed reaffirmation that God indeed cares about marriage, not as a human contract, but as a divine covenant.

Review By
DONRAE MISTRY
October 2025.

About the Author

The author of this book, Daniel Ukadike Nwaelene, ThD, had Christian parents. His father was a Baptist schoolteacher and later the full-time pastor of a Baptist church. His wife – the mother of the author – was a stay-at-home mother, a daughter of one of the foremost deacons of Pilgrim Baptist Church in Nigeria.

The author had his primary (or elementary) and secondary (High School) education in Christian (Baptist) schools. He professed faith in Christ at age eleven by the grace of God. His growth and Christian maturity were gradual, serving the Lord in different capacities in two other churches in the Nigerian Baptist Convention before answering the call to the pastoral ministry.

The author worked briefly in the Federal Civil Service before switching to the pharmaceutical manufacturing industry, where he rose over a period of over two decades, to the post of Division General Manager. He went through Baptist Theologic al Seminary for a four-year Bachelor's degree in Theology (B.Th.), followed later in the USA with a Master of Theology (ThM) and Doctor of Theology (ThD) in Pastoral Theology. He is one of the four ordained ministers (Associate Pastors) in Community Baptist Church, Yonkers, NY, USA., and has pre viously published three books between 2017 and 2020 (both dates inclusive). He has many videos of sermons on his YouTube channel and other social media.

Prior to relocating to the USA, the author pastored Royal Priesthood Baptist Church, Aseese, Ogun State (near Lagos), Nigeria. He began preaching into YouTube as a means of propagating the gospel of Christ during the COVID 19 pandemic stay-at-home restriction periods of 2020 but has continued till date even after the COVID restrictions have been lifted.

The author, Rev. Dr. Daniel U. Nwaelene has been married to Patricia for forty-five years (in this year of writing) and they have been blessed with children and grandchildren to the glory of God.